ALL ABOUT
DINOSAURS

David Lambert

Designed by David Nash

Illustrators
John Francis
Bernard Robinson   Ross Wardle

NUTMEG PRESS

Two boneheads bang heads together in a fight. Each head is armed with knobs and spikes. But neither animal is likely to crack the other's skull. For these big, dome-shaped heads are largely made of solid bone. There is little room for brain inside.

Scientists have dug up the remains of these strange dinosaurs. We know these creatures lived more than 65 million years ago.

CONTENTS

Ages of the Earth

Billions of years ago the Earth was a ball of burning rock and gas. There was no life of any kind. Then the rocks cooled and a flood of rain formed the oceans. In these ancient oceans the first living things appeared. They were no more than tiny blobs of jelly.

As millions of years passed, more and more animals and plants appeared, each kind different from the last. As new kinds of animals appeared, so some of the old ones died out. But all the animals that live today and all the animals that lived before came from the first tiny sea creatures.

Scientists divide the story of life on Earth into ages, or eras. These eras are divided into shorter spans of time called periods. The chart below shows the eras and periods with some of the animals and plants that lived at the time.

The Paleozoic Era is the age of ancient life. When it began, about 600 million years ago, there were already living things in the sea. By the time the era ended plants and animals had invaded the land.

The Mesozoic Era is the middle age of life. In Mesozoic times, dinosaurs and other reptiles ruled the land, the air and the sea. The Mesozoic Era is sometimes called the Age of Dinosaurs.

The Cenozoic Era is the era of recent life. It began about 65 million years ago, after the dinosaurs had died out. During the Cenozoic Era mammals came to rule the Earth.

Human beings appeared on Earth about one million years ago. Our history is very short compared with the history of other animals. But human beings have come to rule the world in a way that no other animal ever did before.

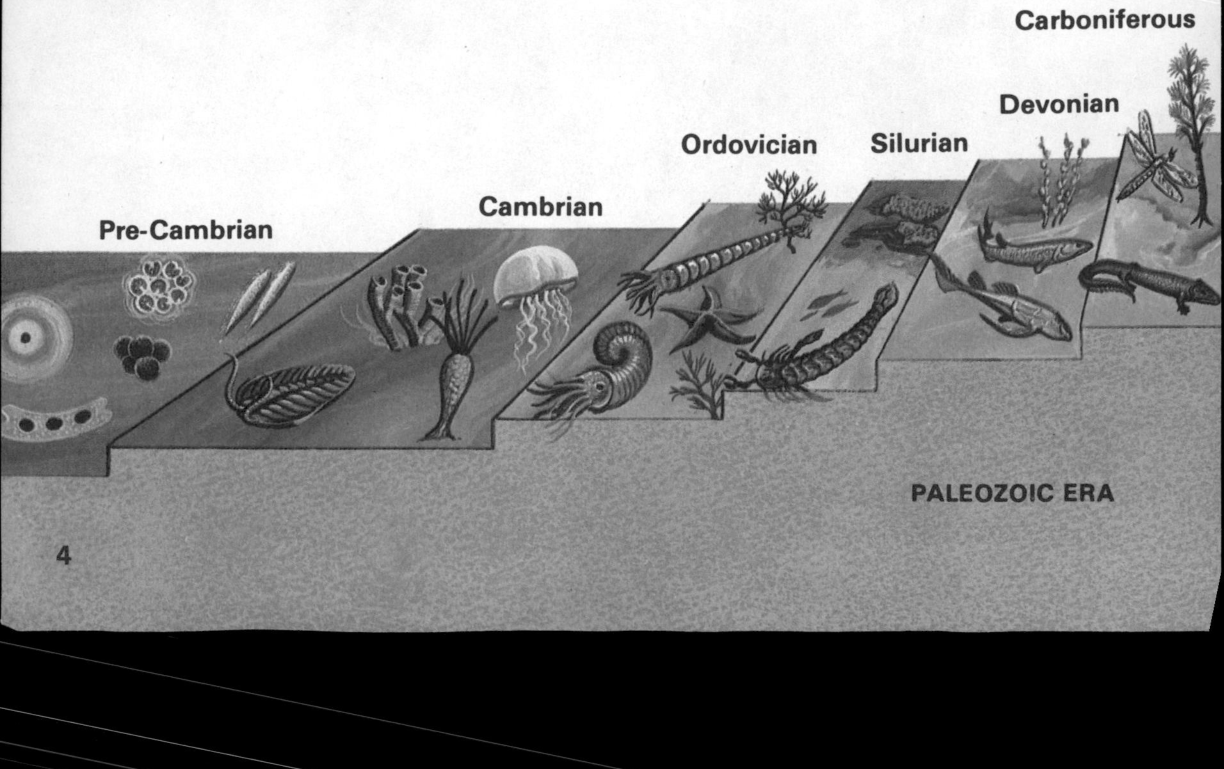

Carboniferous

Devonian

Ordovician   Silurian

Cambrian

Pre-Cambrian

PALEOZOIC ERA

4

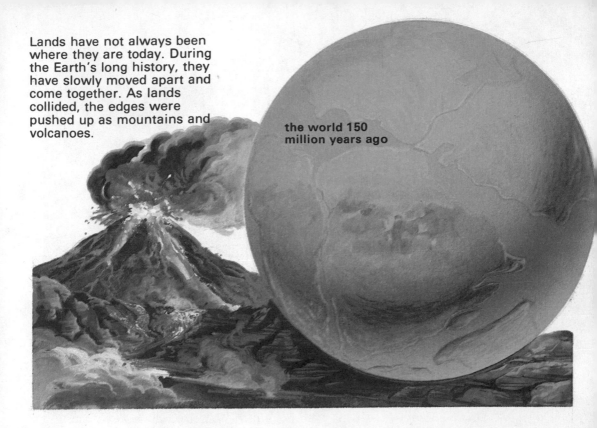

Lands have not always been where they are today. During the Earth's long history, they have slowly moved apart and come together. As lands collided, the edges were pushed up as mountains and volcanoes.

the world 150 million years ago

Permian

Triassic

Jurassic

Cretaceous

Tertiary

Quaternary

MESOZOIC ERA

CENOZOIC ERA

The first amphibians evolved from fishes like the one below. It had lungs to breathe air and fins almost long enough to walk on. Some young fishes were probably the first creatures to find that life was better close to the land. By the water's edge, there were plants and insects for them to eat. And there was no danger from bigger fishes. As time passed, the young fishes would go farther from the water and spend more and more time on land.

Eusthenopteron

A New Life on Land

Think how bare the Earth must have looked with no plants to make it green. Plants did not grow on land until the Paleozoic Era was half over. But as soon as they did, it meant that animals could live on land, too, because there would be food for them.

The first big land animals were amphibians. They ate insects on land and fishes in the water. They may even have eaten the plants. The first amphibians were not much more than fishes which spent part of their lives on land.

Ichthyostega in the picture had a tail with a fin like a fish, but it had lungs for breathing like a land animal. Its skin was soft and had to be kept moist, and it could only lay its eggs in water. So it could never stray far from its pool.

At the time when *Ichthyostega* lived, the land was so swampy that there was no real reason for animals to learn to live on dry land.

When Reptiles Ruled

Amphibians can breathe, feed and move around on land. But their damp skins dry up unless kept moist. So do the small, soft eggs they lay. This means that they must always return to the water to breed.

The first backboned creatures to spend all their time out of water were reptiles. They developed from amphibians about 280 million years ago. The reptiles had strong legs and could move more easily on land than the clumsy amphibians. They had thick, waterproof skins to prevent their bodies from drying up. And they laid eggs with hard, waterproof shells.

There were so many reptiles in the Mesozoic Era that it has become known as the Age of Reptiles. For nearly 200 million years, reptiles ruled the world.

There were plant-eating reptiles much larger than elephants. There were meat-eating reptiles as tall as giraffes, with long, jagged teeth.

And there were reptiles covered with bony armor.

One of the strangest of these creatures was *Dimetrodon*, a reptile with long spikes jutting from its back. A web of skin was stretched between these spikes. It looked like a tall sail. *Dimetrodon's* sail was probably used as a radiator. Body heat lost from the big surface of the sail would have helped *Dimetrodon* to keep cool in the hot sun.

Dimetrodon used its sharp teeth to kill and eat amphibians as well as other reptiles. The picture shows *Dimetrodon* fighting *Ophiacodon*, another meat-eating reptile that was bigger than a man. *Dimetrodon's* young are hatching from their eggs in the front of the picture.

The first reptiles were small, sharp-toothed beasts with rather short legs. They probably crept around on all fours in swampy forests, eating insects and small amphibians.

Later, there were reptiles with longer legs. These helped them to move easily and quickly. Some developed long, strong hind limbs. One of these animals was *Euparkeria.* It lived about 210 million years ago. When *Euparkeria* was in a hurry it ran almost upright on its hind legs. A long tail helped to keep its balance. It probably chased and ate flying insects.

The Gentle Giants

From small, fast-moving reptiles came the early dinosaurs. Some of these grew to enormous sizes. The biggest, the sauropods, were the largest animals that have ever lived on land.

A long neck and tail jutted from the sauropod's huge, barrel-shaped body. It lumbered around on legs much larger than an elephant's.

Sauropods were gentle giants. They browsed on twigs and leaves. They may have moved around in herds, keeping their young in the middle for safety.

The picture shows three kinds of sauropods. Nearby stands a munching *Brontosaurus*. *Brontosaurus* weighed as much as six elephants. It was so heavy that people once imagined the ground shaking and rumbling as it lumbered along. The *Brontosaurus* in the picture has a scarred hide. Even these giants were not safe from the claws and teeth of the meat-eating dinosaurs.

Beyond *Brontosaurus* stalks a *Barosaurus*. With its extra-long neck it could feed on leaves from the very tops of the trees.

In the distance, a small herd of *Diplodocus* browses beside a lake. *Diplodocus* was the longest land animal ever. From its tiny head to the tip of its long tail, *Diplodocus* measured up to 88 feet (27 meters).

Terrible Lizards

The name dinosaur means "terrible lizard." Dinosaurs were not lizards at all, but some would certainly have been terrible to meet. These were the big meat-eaters who killed and fed upon the plant-eating dinosaurs. Some stood as high as a giraffe. But there were also meat-eaters no bigger than a chicken. These ate insects.

Among the most terrifying of the giant dinosaurs was *Tyrannosaurus rex*, or "king of the tyrant lizards." *Tyrannosaurus* ran upright on its powerful hind legs. It grabbed its victims with its deadly hind claws and tore at their flesh with teeth as big and sharp as daggers. How *Tyrannosaurus* used its tiny front legs is a mystery. They were too small even to help cram food into the reptile's great jaws.

In the picture a herd of duck-billed dinosaurs is fleeing in terror from a hungry *Tyrannosaurus*. Duckbills were harmless dinosaurs. They munched leaves with jaws that ended in a duck-like beak. Some duckbills had hollow crests on their heads. These crests were connected to their nostrils and may have given the duckbills a keen sense of smell. This would have helped the reptiles find food, and it warned them of approaching enemies.

Parasaurolophus

Ornithomimus raiding a nest of eggs. This meat-eating dinosaur was the shape and size of an ostrich. But it had limbs with claws instead of wings.

Armored Dinosaurs

Most plant-eating dinosaurs were timid creatures. They ran away when the fierce meat-eating dinosaurs attacked. But others stood their ground. They had armor plating to protect their bodies.

Stegosaurus was among the first of these armored beasts. It was as long as a bus and walked on its four sturdy legs. Two rows of bony plates jutted out from its back like broad spear blades. And two pairs of spikes guarded its tail. But the sides of this odd creature were not well protected. *Stegosaurus* might have swung its spiked tail like a club, but it was no match for the giant meat-eaters. Dinosaurs with better armor survived after *Stegosaurus* died out.

Ankylosaurus was a very well armored dinosaur. It was as long as *Stegosaurus*. But its low, flat back was completely covered with bony armor. Bony shields guarded its head. Bony spikes jutted from its sides. And a bony ring enclosed its tail. The tip of its tail made a big bony club. *Ankylosaurus* was built for defense.

Some armored dinosaurs were built for attack as well as defense. There were horned dinosaurs as large as elephants. *Triceratops* had three long horns sprouting from its massive head, and a broad bony frill protected its neck. Even *Tyrannosaurus* may have retreated when an angry *Triceratops* charged.

Ankylosaurus

14

Stegosaurus

Triceratops

In Air and Sea

When dinosaurs roamed the land, other strange reptiles ruled the air and the sea.

Most of the creatures of the air were reptiles called pterosaurs, or "winged lizards." They had wings of leathery skin stretched between their long front legs and their short back legs. Pterosaurs hung awkwardly like bats from cliffs and trees. But they could swoop and glide splendidly.

Rhamphorhynchus had a rudder at the end of its long tail to help

Pteranodon

Ichthyosaurus

Elasmosaurus

it steer. It glided near the water. Now and then, it swooped to snatch up fish with the sharp teeth in its long jaws.

Pteranodon's body was no bigger than a turkey's. But its great wings would have spread across a freeway. *Pteranodon* soared over the sea and snatched fish in its big toothless jaws.

Swimming reptiles hunted in the water. *Ichthyosaurus* had fins and flippers instead of legs. It looked and swam like a dolphin. *Elasmosaurus* was a giant of the seas, with a long, snake-like neck.

Rhamphorhynchus

a small plesiosaur

a family of
early mammals

18

The End of an Era

Towards the end of the Mesozoic Era, dinosaurs and other giant reptiles were masters of the land, the seas and the skies. The rule of the reptiles had lasted for 150 million years. Then something strange happened. Quite suddenly all of these great creatures died out. When the Mesozoic Era came to an end the largest reptile left alive was the crocodile.

Why this happened is a mystery. Some people once thought that dinosaurs died by eating new plants which poisoned them. Other people believed that the great reptiles were killed by disease. Yet another idea was that tiny shrew-like animals ate the dinosaurs' eggs.

Archaeopteryx, the first known bird

Now, most scientists think that the dinosaurs were killed by cold. After millions of years of mild weather the climates of the world grew cold. Like modern reptiles, the dinosaurs had no fur to keep their bodies warm. And they were much too big to find shelter. Pterosaurs could not fly in winter gales, and the great sea reptiles died as the warm seas grew cold.

The death of the dinosaurs meant a new chance for creatures which survived the cold. Fish once again became masters of the sea. Birds replaced the flying reptiles as masters of the skies. And small, furry creatures which had been on Earth almost as long as the dinosaurs became rulers of the land. From these little animals developed all of the mammals that live on Earth today.

the crocodile, the largest living reptile

Stories in Stone

No person has ever seen a living dinosaur. The dinosaurs died out many millions of years before the first human beings appeared on Earth. We only know about these ancient creatures from fossils.

When animals die, their bodies normally rot. But sometimes their bones are preserved as fossils. One way in which an animal can be fossilized is shown at the top of the page. Suppose a prehistoric creature such as *Iguanodon* died by falling off a cliff into the sea. Its skin and soft flesh would soon rot, but its skeleton would sink to the bottom and be covered by sand.

Slowly, over millions of years, this sand would harden into solid rock. The bones, locked inside the rock, would also harden. Millions of years later, the rocks may become dry land, and as they are worn away the skeleton can be seen.

People who collect and study fossils are called paleontologists. The paleontologist in the picture below has found the skeleton of *Iguanodon* in the rocks. She is very

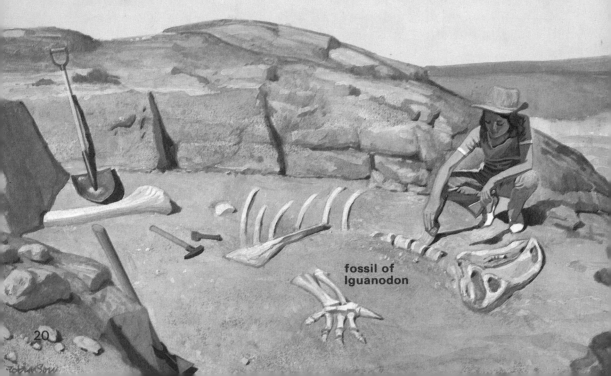

fossil of
Iguanodon

careful as she chips and brushes the rock from around the bones. When she has removed all the bones she will be able to wire them together to make a stone skeleton of the animal. She will be able to tell what the creature ate from the shape of its teeth, how it stood and ran from its feet, and much more.

reconstructed
skeleton of
Iguanodon

Parasaurolophus

Tyrannosaurus

Brontosaurus

Man

Ornithomimus

Stegosaurus

Compsognathus

23

A Dictionary of Dinosaurs

Allosaurus was a huge, meat-eating dinosaur. It ran on powerful hind legs.

Ankylosaurus was one of the most heavily armored dinosaurs, with bony plates and spikes covering its head, back, and tail.

Barosaurus was a long-necked dinosaur. It browsed on the leaves of trees.

Brachiosaurus resembled Brontosaurus but was even larger. It was the largest land animal ever to live on Earth.

Brontosaurus was a huge plant-eating dinosaur.

Camptosaurus was an ornithopod which fed mainly on the juicy leaves of trees.

Ceratopsians were a group of horned, plant-eating dinosaurs.

Compognathus, no larger than a turkey, was one of the smallest dinosaurs.

Corythosaurus was a duckbill dinosaur, with a helmet-like crest on its head.

Dinosaur is the name given to the great extinct land reptiles belonging to the Saurischian and Ornithischian orders.

Diplodocus was the longest of the dinosaurs. It measured 88 feet (27 meters) from head to tail.

Hadrosaurs were a group of dinosaurs with broad, toothless beaks.

Heterodontosaurus was a little reptile barely larger than a goose.

Iguanodon was a plant-eating ornithopod. It ran on its hind legs.

Ophiacodon was an early meat-eater.

Ornithischians formed one of the two great groups of dinosaurs. All were plant-eaters. The other great group of dinosaurs were the Saurischians.

Ornithomimus was the shape and size of an ostrich. It probably stole eggs from the nests of other reptiles.

Ornithopods were a group of plant-eating reptiles which walked on their hind legs.

Pachycephalosaurus was one of the group of dinosaurs nicknamed "boneheads."

Parasaurolophus was one of the plant-eating duckbill dinosaurs.

Plateosaurus was an early plant-eater which moved about slowly on all fours.

Saurischians formed one of the two great groups of dinosaurs. They included the gigantic sauropods, such as Brachiosaurus, and the fearsome flesh-eaters, such as Tyrannosaurus. The other great group of dinosaurs was the Ornithischians.

Sauropods were a group of gigantic, plant-eating dinosaurs with huge bodies, long necks, and tiny heads, such as Brontosaurus and Diplodocus. The sauropods must have spent nearly all their time feeding.

Stegosaurus was an armored dinosaur. It had bony plates on its back and spikes on its tail.

Styracosaurus was a horned dinosaur with a spiked collar around its neck. Styracosaurus was one of the last dinosaurs.

Triceratops was an armored dinosaur with three long horns on its head and a bony frill around its neck.

Tyrannosaurus was the largest of the fearsome flesh-eating dinosaurs.